SPECIAL DAYS
Spring

Liz Gogerly

W
FRANKLIN WATTS
LONDON•SYDNEY

SPECIAL DAYS

Titles in this series:

Autumn
Spring
Summer
Winter

© 2004 Arcturus Publishing

Produced for Franklin Watts by Arcturus Publishing Ltd, 26/27 Bickels Yard, 151–153 Bermondsey Street, London SE1 3HA.

Concept: Alex Woolf
Editor: Cath Senker
Designer: Tim Mayer
Picture researcher: Shelley Noronha, Glass Onion Pictures

Published in the UK by Franklin Watts.

A CIP catalogue record for this book is available from the British Library.

ISBN 07496 5457 0

Printed in Italy.

Franklin Watts – the Watts Publishing Group, 96 Leonard Street, London EC2A 4XD.

Picture Acknowledgements:
AI Pictures (all credited to Superbild) cover (top left), 4, 5, 7, 16; Camera Press 10, 11; Chapel Studios (Zul Mukhida) 20; Corbis (Roger Ressmeyer) 27; James Davis Worldwide 29; Eye Ubiquitous (Leon Schadeburg) 17; Sonia Halliday (both David Silverman) 13, 23; Hutchison (John Hatt) 8; Impact (Robin Laurance) 6; Popperfoto (Reuters/Fabrizio Bensch) 18; David Silverman cover (top right), 12, 26; Topham (all credited to The Image Works) (Lee Snider) cover (bottom right), (Michael Siluk) 19, (Lee Snider) 25, (Michael Doolittle) 28; World Religions Photo Library (Kapoor) cover (top centre), (Gapper) cover (bottom left), (Christine Osborne) cover (bottom centre), (Kapoor) 9, (C. Osborne) 14, (Gapper) 15, (C. Osborne) 21, (C. Osborne) 22, (Barton) 24.

Cover pictures (clockwise from top left): The Prophet's birthday, Holi, Purim, the Easter Parade, Wesak and Vaisakhi.

Note:
The quotations in this book are fictionalized accounts drawn from factual sources.

Contents

Note: When Muslims say the name of one of the Prophets, they say 'Peace Be Upon Him' afterwards. This is shown in Arabic as ﷺ in this book.

Celebrating New Life

After the long, cold winter people are delighted to see the first signs of spring. Buds on plants and trees are growing and will soon turn into new leaves. Spring flowers are opening and bringing colour back into all our lives. In the fields, lambs are playing. It's like the whole world is being woken up and new life is being born.

At this spring festival in Switzerland people wear traditional clothes and gather fresh flowers.

People have celebrated the coming of spring since ancient times. On the **spring equinox** on March 21 there was feasting and dancing. Today, many spring festivals are good fun. During the Hindu festival of Holi, people squirt each other with coloured water. On St Patrick's Day, there are massive street parades in the USA, with people wearing items of green clothing. And, for the Jewish festival of Purim, children go to fancy-dress parties. Many countries celebrate New Year during spring with parties and fireworks.

A street parade in Savannah, Georgia in the USA. Irish people all over the world celebrate St Patrick's Day.

This book looks at festivals during the spring months in the **northern hemisphere**. On the other side of the world – in countries such as Australia and New Zealand – it's autumn then. Remember that in **tropical** regions, such as parts of Thailand, it may be warm all year round.

Liam's St Patrick's Day

'Everything turns green on St Patrick's Day. All the family picks something green to wear – once I dressed up as a leprechaun (a naughty elf). There's a big parade in town but we have our own party at home. Mom puts green food colouring in the muffins and lemonade so our tongues turn green too!'
Liam, New York, USA

Ashura and Milad an-Nabi

The Muslim year is shorter than the Western calendar year. Muslim festivals take place on the same date each year in the Muslim calendar, but change according to the Western calendar. Ashura and Milad an-Nabi can occur in any season.

The festival of Ashura **commemorates** the death of Muhammad's grandson, Hussain ﷺ. During a battle in 680 CE, Hussain ﷺ was brutally murdered alongside his family and followers near Karbala, in present-day Iraq.

Today, some Muslims remember this tragic event by gathering at the mosque (their place of worship) to pray. In some countries, such as Iraq and Pakistan, there are processions through the streets. People carry models of Hussain's tomb and act out the story of his death. Some people **fast** or give money to charity.

Muslims taking part in a procession at Ashura in Pakistan. In the background you can see a model of Hussain's tomb.

6

Hakim's Milad an–Nabi

'The birthday of the Prophet Muhammad ﷺ is a public holiday in Kenya and many shops are closed. We go to the mosque to pray and read a poem called the Burdah. Later, my mother makes a big meal for all the family and we're given some sweets.'

Hakim, Mombasa, Kenya

Milad an–Nabi

This is the birthday of the **Prophet** Muhammad ﷺ. It's a day of celebration for many Muslims but because Muhammad ﷺ also died on this day it is a time of sadness too. People join together at the mosque to pray and give thanks for his life. They read stories about Muhammad ﷺ and later they might join a procession and eat a special meal. Not all Muslims celebrate this festival.

In Kenya, Africa, many Muslims, such as these boys at a mosque, observe the Prophet's birthday.

Holi, February or March

The Hindu spring festival of Holi is also known as the festival of colour. Holi isn't a religious festival but it is a time when Hindus celebrate new life.

The festival begins on Holi Eve (*Puno*), when a bonfire is lit. The huge, crackling fire is exciting to watch but it also has a special meaning. As the old wood on the fire burns away, it makes way for new growth.

Sometimes, a model of the wicked demon Holika is also burned. Some people dance around the fire to celebrate good winning over evil.

Holi is a time for fun and dancing. These festivities in Jodhpur in India will go on long into the night.

8

The following day (*Parva*), people put on their old clothes and take to the streets with pots of *gullal* (coloured powder) and their water pistols. For a few mad hours people run around smearing *gullal* on each other, soaking everyone with coloured water or bursting balloons filled with dye. There is colour everywhere!

When the fun dies down, people return home to clean up and put on their best clothes. Then the celebrations continue with a tasty vegetarian feast, followed by music and dancing.

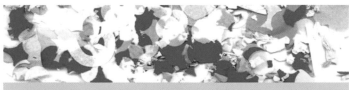

Deepa's Holi

'In our village we put up two wooden poles near the temple. On Holi Eve we light a bonfire near the poles and dance. The next day there is a procession to the temple. My favourite part of Holi is throwing rice and turmeric (a yellow spice) at people. Sometimes we dress up or put on animal masks and go from house to house collecting money for charity.'
Deepa, Kerala, India

Hindu children look forward to celebrating Holi and covering everyone with coloured powder.

Mother's Day, March

On Mother's Day, children of all ages can show their mother how much they love her. By giving her cards, flowers and gifts they make her feel special.

There is a long history of Mother's Day that probably goes back to ancient times. The ancient Greeks held a festival in spring to honour Rhea, the mother goddess. Later, the ancient Romans worshipped the goddess Cybele.

The first time people put aside a day for their own mothers was in Britain in the seventeenth century. Mothering Sunday was held on the fourth Sunday in **Lent**. In those days, people often worked seven days a week, but Mothering Sunday was a day off for everybody. They returned home with small gifts or cake.

Mothers like to receive a bunch of flowers on Mother's Day. They also like it when you make them a special present or card.

Jodie's Mother's Day

'I get up really early so I can surprise my mum with breakfast and flowers in bed – she always loves that. Later we go out to my auntie's house for a meal with all the family. My grandma and my great-grandma are always there and we give them flowers too.'
Jodie, Aberdeen, UK

Breakfast in bed is a lovely surprise for your mum. It's even better if you clear up afterwards!

Mother's Day began in the USA because of a woman called Anna M. Jarvis. For many years, she campaigned for a national holiday on Mother's Day. In May 1905 Anna's own mother died. On the anniversary of Anna's mother's death, in May 1908, a special Mother's Day ceremony was held at her mother's church in Grafton, West Virginia. The idea caught on and in 1913 Mother's Day became a national holiday.

11

Purim, February or March

Purim is one of the liveliest festivals in the Jewish calendar. Children particularly like Purim because they can dress up and make lots of noise – even in their place of worship, the synagogue!

On the eve of Purim, Jews meet at the synagogue to listen to readings from the *Megillah* of Esther (the Book of Esther). They hear the story of how a young Jewish girl called Esther saved the Jews of Persia (present-day Iran) from Haman, the King's wicked and greedy prime minister.

In the weeks leading up to Purim, people are busy making costumes. They dress up as characters from the Book of Esther or other people from Jewish history.

Julian's Purim

'Mum and Dad always tell me that it is important that we help people who are less well off than we are. At Purim the synagogue organizes collections of food, clothing and money to give away to the needy. I give some of my old books and toys too. I like dressing up and having fun at Purim but I think it's really good to remember others too.'

Julian, Paris, France

The next day everybody returns to the synagogue to listen to the *Megillah* again. This time, some of the **congregation** might dress up as characters from the story. To add to the fun, the congregation hisses or boos when Haman is mentioned. People shake rattles, known as *graggers* or *ra'ashanim* (Purim noisemakers).

Later that day there are fancy-dress parties and plays about the story of Esther. Special meals are prepared and as a treat for children there are delicious triangular-shaped *hamantaschen* cakes, often filled with jam or nuts.

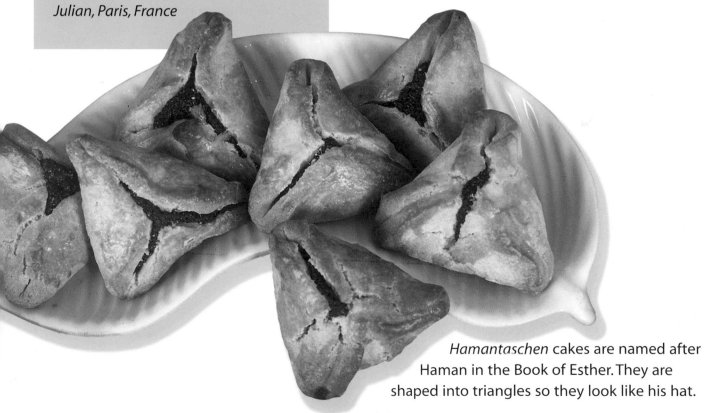

Hamantaschen cakes are named after Haman in the Book of Esther. They are shaped into triangles so they look like his hat.

13

Vaisakhi, April

At Vaisakhi Sikhs celebrate their New Year. They remember the founding of the *Khalsa*, the Sikh community, by **Guru** Gobind Singh. Throughout India it is also the beginning of harvest time so it is a day for thanksgiving and celebration.

Guru Gobind Singh founded the *Khalsa* in 1699. He asked five volunteers to risk their lives in a test of faith. They became the first members of the *Khalsa*.

Nowadays, celebrations begin with a procession headed by the 'Five Beloved', who represent those first members of the *Khalsa*. They are dressed in yellow robes and carry swords. Another important ceremony is the taking down and washing of the flag, the *Nishan Sahib*, outside each Sikh temple. Afterwards there are prayers and readings.

A crowd of Sikhs watch as the washed flag is raised outside their temple in London, UK.

Gurdeep's Vaisakhi

'When we perform *bhangra* we are telling the story of the farming year. We mime out ploughing, sowing and reaping. Then we really let go and celebrate the harvest. We move to the beat of the *dholak* (drum)… the dancing is hard work, and your legs burn – but it's a cool thing!'
Gurdeep, Chicago, USA

The celebrations continue with feasts, parties or fairs. Groups of men dressed in brightly coloured clothes perform *bhangra*. This traditional folk dancing began in the Punjab (part of India and Pakistan) to celebrate the harvest. Now it is one of the most enjoyable parts of Vaisakhi for Sikhs everywhere. They stay up late into the night singing, playing music and joining in the dancing.

Sikh men performing *bhangra* dancing to the rhythm of traditional drums in the streets of London, UK.

Songkran – Thai New Year, April

In April, people all over Thailand celebrate the Buddhist New Year festival of Songkran. As well as welcoming in the New Year, they give thanks for the health and happiness in their lives.

Water fights are one of the highlights of the celebrations during Songkran.

Water is a symbol of cleansing, and during Songkran everybody is prepared to get wet. The first day marks the end of the old year. In the morning, people visit the Buddhist temple, bringing gifts to the monks.

Dancing in the streets of Chiang Mai. Floats with Buddha images are paraded through the streets too.

Afterwards, **Buddha** images are bathed in water. Young people pour scented water on to the hands of elders and parents to show them respect.

The following day, people clean their houses and throw away old things. Later, they go into the streets to shower each other with water from buckets, water-pistols and hoses. There are boat races and processions.

Kusa's Songkran

'In April everybody feels hot and it's hard to concentrate at school. Then the holiday of Songkran begins and we all wake up. I enjoy the water-fights. We go out on the back of a truck with buckets of water. It's best when you splash motorcyclists or people with the windows down in their cars. It's so hot that nobody minds if they get wet.'
Kusa, Chiang Mai, Thailand

The third day, Songkran Day, is New Year's Day. People dress up and visit the temple. All over Thailand, people have different ways of celebrating. There will be music and dancing, puppet shows and processions, fireworks, fairs and feasts. Many people release fish or caged birds.

Days to Remember

Some special days commemorate events or people from the past. They are a good time to think about how we live our lives.

On Holocaust **Memorial** Day (January in the UK; April in the United States) people remember the millions who died in Nazi **death camps** during World War II. Plays, concerts, and exhibitions are put on to teach people about the Holocaust.

Memorial Day

The last Monday in May is Memorial Day. People attend special church services to remember all the servicemen and women who have died serving their country. The first Memorial Day was held in 1868 to honor soldiers killed in the Civil War. After World War I, Memorial Day became a day of remembrance for Americans killed or missing in action in all wars.

Lighting candles is one way to remember those killed during the Holocaust. Here, children in Berlin, Germany, have formed the words "fight back."

18

Cinco de Mayo

The Cinco de Mayo (May 5) festival is colorful and exciting. It commemorates the Mexican victory over France at the Battle of Puebla in 1862. In Mexico and in parts of the United States, people decorate the streets with Mexican flags. Everyone dances to Mexican music and eats Mexican food.

Children enjoy the celebrations in Minnesota. There may also be fireworks and dancing.

Benito's Cinco de Mayo

"Every year the people in my neighborhood get together to act out the battle of 1862. Some people play the French invaders while the rest play the Mexicans who won the battle. In some places they use real guns for the performance but we throw fruit at each other instead!"

Benito, Mexico City, Mexico

Wesak, May or June

For many Buddhists, Wesak (sometimes called **Buddha** Day) is the most sacred festival in the Buddhist calendar. On this special day they celebrate the birth, **Enlightenment** and death of the Buddha. They believe that all three events happened on the same day, yet in different years, so it is an anniversary celebration.

Throughout the world, Wesak is celebrated in many different ways. Buddhists generally gather at their local temples and **monasteries**. These holy places are decorated with beautiful fresh flowers and streamers. An important part of the celebration is joining together to pray, chant and listen to stories about the life of Buddha.

Young Buddhists bring baskets of flowers and food as offerings to the monks at this temple in the UK.

There is also a 'Bathing of the Buddha' ceremony in which scented water is poured over an image of the Buddha. Some people place **offerings** of fruit, sweets and flowers beside a statue of the Buddha to show respect for his teachings. They also send each other special cards or gifts.

Dinusha's Wesak

'During Wesak I like to go into town to see what's going on. Usually, the streets are decorated with paintings of the life of Buddha. There are lights everywhere too – lanterns, coloured bulbs and tiny coconut oil lamps. There are pantomimes and plays and sometimes there are rock bands playing.'
Dinusha, Colombo, Sri Lanka

A young monk washes the statue of Buddha in the temple at Yangon in Burma. It is one of the most important Wesak rituals.

Each country celebrates Wesak in its own way too. In China, there are processions with traditional dancing dragons. In Thailand, people clean their homes and release caged birds to represent freedom. In Sri Lanka, people wear white clothes.

21

Holy Week Begins,
MARCH OR APRIL

Easter might simply mean chocolate eggs to many people. For Christians, it is a time to remember the last week in Jesus' life. Holy Week is the last week of Lent, leading up to Easter Sunday.

Holy Week begins on Palm Sunday, when Christians remember how Jesus entered Jerusalem on a donkey. Crowds of people welcomed him into the town by waving palm branches. To mark this day, churches are decorated with palm leaves, and members of the congregation hold small palm crosses. People sing hymns and listen to readings from the Bible.

Elena's Palm Sunday

"On Palm Sunday, we go to **mass** in the morning. All the children carry palm leaves, which have been blessed by the priest. The boys' palm leaves don't have decorations, but the girls decorate theirs with candy, flowers, tinsel, or whatever looks pretty."

Elena, Seville, Spain

The congregation holds palm leaves for the Palm Sunday procession in a village in Ghana.

Priests in Jerusalem, Israel, take part in a foot-washing ceremony on Maundy Thursday.

Maundy Thursday commemorates the Last Supper, when Jesus ate the traditional **Passover** meal with his twelve disciples, or followers. He told them that the wine and the bread represented his blood and body. He then washed their feet to show them that all people are the same. This was the day when Judas betrayed Jesus.

Many churches hold foot-washing ceremonies on Maundy Thursday. It reminds people that as well as serving others, they should allow others to serve them. Some churches give Maundy gifts. Since the thirteenth century, British kings and queens have given special silver Maundy coins to people in need.

Good Friday and Easter Sunday, March or April

The most solemn day in Holy Week is Good Friday, the anniversary of when Jesus died on the cross. It seems strange to call such a sad day 'Good Friday', but it reminds Christians of the good that came from the events of Holy Week. In Germany, this day is called *Karfreitag*, which translates as Mourning Friday, or Silent Friday.

On Good Friday, church services focus on Jesus' suffering on the cross. In some countries there are Good Friday processions, and people dress up and act out the last week of Jesus' life in 'passion plays'. In Britain, people eat hot cross buns. The currants in the buns represent the nails in the cross and the spices are for tears and sadness. The cross on top is a symbol of the cross on which Jesus died.

In Latin America many people hold special Good Friday processions. These men in Antigua, Guatemala, are helping to carry a huge float with a giant model of Jesus and his cross.

A family wearing Easter bonnets taking part in the Easter Parade in New York, USA.

Michael's Easter Sunday

'I gave up chocolate for Lent. Can you believe it, no chocolate for over forty days? Some of my friends at school thought it was strange but the chocolate eggs I ate on Easter Sunday tasted even more delicious because I hadn't had chocolate for so long!'

Michael, Frankfurt, Germany

Easter Sunday

Easter Sunday is a joyous day when Christians remember how Jesus rose from the dead. Churches everywhere are decorated with fresh flowers and **paschal candles** are lit. Later in the day, children receive chocolate Easter eggs, which represent new life and hope. There is more fun with Easter parades, Easter bonnet competitions and egg hunts.

Passover, March or April

The Jewish festival of Passover, known as *Pesach* in Hebrew, celebrates the time when the Israelites, the people of Israel, were saved from slavery by Moses. Passover also marks the beginning of the barley harvest in Israel.

Seder night brings all the family together, and everyone helps to read aloud from the *Hagadah*. On the table is a plate with some of the symbols of Passover.

The story of Passover begins more than 3,000 years ago. When the Israelites fled Egypt they left in a rush. There was no time to bake bread. As they traveled through the desert they survived on flat bread that hadn't risen, called *matzo*.

The father shares *matzo* as part of the ceremony.

Eliana's Seder night

"On Seder night we eat foods that help us think about how the children of Israel suffered. The horseradish tastes bitter—it makes my eyes run. We also eat parsley and hard-boiled eggs because they represent spring. We dip them in salt water to remind us of the tears of the Jews."

Eliana, Tel Aviv, Israel

Egyptian soldiers followed the Israelites as far as the Red Sea. Just when it seemed the Israelites would be captured, the sea parted, allowing them to cross. When the Egyptians tried to follow, the waves crashed over them. It was a miracle and the story is retold every Passover.

Throughout the eight days of Passover, Jews eat *matzo* instead of ordinary bread, to remind them of the Israelites' suffering. The Seder, at the start of Passover, is the most important event. On Seder night, family and friends gather to read from the *Hagadah*, the book that tells the story of Passover. As part of the ceremony, everyone enjoys a delicious meal, and afterward there are games and songs.

27

May Day, 1 May

The happy holiday of May Day goes back to ancient times. The ancient Romans honoured Flora, the goddess of flowers and springtime. On the eve of May Day, people in ancient Britain celebrated Beltane (Bright Fire). They welcomed in summer with **sacrifices** and feasts. They also lit bonfires for young men to leap over. It was said that the following year's crops would grow as high as they jumped.

These children in New Haven, Connecticut, USA, are dancing around a maypole that has been set up in their school playground.

By medieval times, May Day had become a popular holiday in England. Villagers woke early to go gathering flowers and tree branches to decorate their homes. They put up a maypole on the village green and decked it with flowers and ribbons. The villagers danced around the maypole and played games. A May Queen was chosen to reign over the festivities.

Today, in villages in many parts of the world, maypoles are set up on May Day. Other customs can be fun or romantic. They reflect the joy of new life or new love in the springtime. In Italy, children go looking for the first swallow of spring. Meanwhile Italian men sing love songs to their girlfriends.

May Day celebrations in Hawaii, where May Day is called Lei Day. Everyone gives the gift of a *lei* (garland of flowers) to someone else. As they put the *lei* around the receiver's neck, they give him or her a kiss.

Charlene's Lei Day

'The first of May is **Lei** Day in Hawaii. It's beautiful because everyone is wearing flowers. At school we have a pageant (it's a competition) and a queen is chosen. There are games and prizes for the most beautiful lei. I made mine from flowers, shells, beads and feathers – it looked lovely but I didn't win a prize.'

Charlene, Honolulu, Hawaii

Calendar of Holidays

Most religions follow a lunar calendar, based on the moon's movements, rather than a solar calendar. They adjust the calendar to keep the holidays in their season. Muslims don't adjust their calendar, so the holidays can be at any time of the year and are not related to the seasons. Sikh festivals are usually three days long because they include the two-day reading of the Sikh holy book before the festival day.

2004

Holocaust Day (UK)	January 27
Ashura	March 2
Holi	March 6
Purim	March 7
St Patrick's Day	March 17
Mother's Day (UK)	March 21
Palm Sunday	April 4
Maundy Thursday	April 8
Good Friday	April 9
Easter Sunday	April 11
Passover	April 5–13
Vaisakhi	April 13
Songkran	April 13
Holocaust Day (USA)	April 18
Beltane	April 30
May Day	May 1
Milad an-Nabi	May 2
Cinco de Mayo	April 29–May 4
Mother's Day (USA)	May 9
Memorial Day	May 31
Wesak	June 2

2005

Holocaust Day (UK)	January 27
Ashura	February 19
Holi	February 25
Mother's Day (UK)	March 6
St Patrick's Day	March 17
Palm Sunday	March 20
Maundy Thursday	March 24
Good Friday	March 25
Purim	March 25
Easter Sunday	March 27
Holocaust Day (USA)	April 5
Vaisakhi	April 13
Songkran	April 13
Milad an-Nabi	April 21
Passover	April 23–May 5
Beltane	April 30
May Day	May 1
Cinco de Mayo	May 5–7
Mother's Day (USA)	May 8
Wesak	May 25
Memorial Day	May 30

2006

Holocaust Day (UK)	January 27
Ashura	February 9
Holi	March 14
Purim	March 14
St Patrick's Day	March 17
Mother's Day (UK)	March 26
Palm Sunday	April 9
Milad an-Nabi	April 12
Passover	April 12–20
Vaisakhi	April 13
Songkran	April 13
Maundy Thursday	April 13
Good Friday	April 14
Easter Sunday	April 16
Holocaust Day (USA)	April 25
Beltane	April 30
May Day	May 1
Mother's Day (USA)	May 4
Cinco de Mayo	May 4–6
Wesak	May 13
Memorial Day	May 29

Glossary

Buddha (BOOD uh) The man who founded the Buddhist religion.

commemorate (cuh MEM uh rayt) To do something special to remember an important person or event.

congregation (KON grih gay shun) A group of people gathered at a place of worship.

death camps Camps where the Nazis sent prisoners in World War II. Millions of people were murdered or died from starvation and disease in these camps.

enlightenment (en LYT un ment) When a person has become perfectly kind and generous, understands the world completely, and is fearless.

fast To give up eating food for a time, often for religious reasons.

Guru (guh ROO) Teacher.

lei (LAY) In Hawaii, a garland or necklace of flowers given in welcome or to say goodbye.

Lent The forty days before Easter in the Christian calendar. Many Christians give up a favorite food or activity for Lent.

mass A Roman Catholic religious ceremony in which bread and wine stand for the body and blood of Jesus Christ.

memorial (muh MOR ee ul) A place, an object, or a custom that is set up to help people remember a person or an event.

monasteries (MON uh ster eez) The buildings where monks live.

northern hemisphere (NOR thern HEM uh sfeer) The half of the earth north of the equator.

offerings (OFF uh ringz) Things that are offered in thanks to a god or Prophet.

paschal candles (PASS kul CAN dulz) Candles lit in church on Easter Sunday. The flame represents Jesus rising from the dead as the "light of the world."

Passover (PASS oh ver) A Jewish festival to remember when God rescued the Israelites from Egypt.

Prophet (PROF et) In the Muslim religion, a Prophet is a holy person who brought God's message to the world.

sacrifices (SAK ruh fice uhz) The killing of an animal or person as offerings to a god.

spring equinox (SPRING EH kwe nocks) The equinox happens twice a year when day and night are of equal length. The spring equinox is around March 21 in the northern hemisphere and around September 22 in the southern hemisphere.

tropical (TRAHP uk kul) To do with living in the hot, rainy areas of the tropics.

Further Reading

Breuilly, Elizabeth et al. *Festivals of the World: The Illustrated Guide to Celebrations, Customs, Events and Holidays.* Facts on File, 2002

Cooper, Ilene. *Jewish Holidays All Year Round.* Abrams, 2002

Ganeri, Anita. *Christian Festivals Throughout the Year.* Smart Apple Media, 2003

Gnojewski, Carol. *Cinco de Mayo: Celebrating Hispanic Pride.* Enslow, 2002

Schuh, Mari C. *St. Patrick's Day.* Pebble Books, 2002

Senker, Cath. *My Buddhist Year.* Hodder and Stoughton, 2003

Senker, Cath. *My Muslim Year.* Hodder and Stoughton, 2003

Websites to Visit

www.amaana.org/islam/muslimholidays.htm

www.urbandharma.org/udharma3/holidays.html

www.melizo.com/festivals/

www.aish.com/holidays/

www.kidsdomain.com/holiday/mom

www.mexonline.com/cinco.htm

Index

All numbers in **bold** refer to pictures as well as text.